ALSO BY ELAINE KAHN

A Voluptuous Dream During an Eclipse (Poor Claudia, 2012)
Customer (Ecstatic Peace Library, 2010)
Convinced By the End Of It (Big Baby Books, 2009)
Radiant Bottle Caps (Glasseye Books, 2008)

WOMEN IN PUBLIC

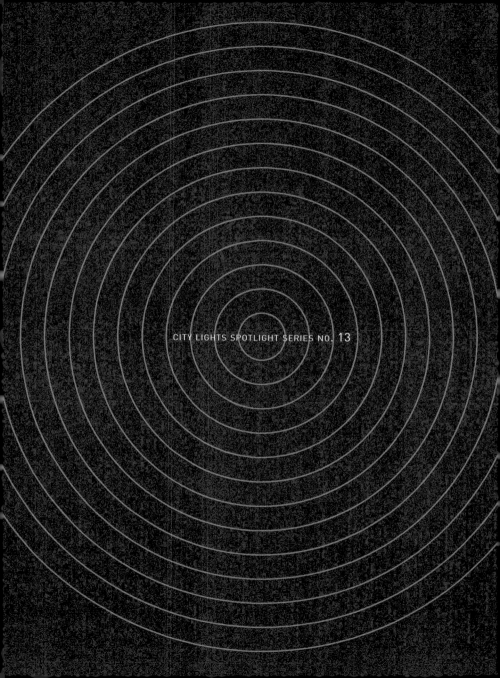

CITY LIGHTS SPOTLIGHT SERIES NO. 13

ELAINE KAHN

WOMEN

IN

PUBLIC

CITY LIGHTS

SAN FRANCISCO

CITY LIGHTS SPOTLIGHT
The City Lights Spotlight Series was founded in 2009,
and is edited by Garrett Caples.

Library of Congress Cataloging-in-Publication Data
on file

Cover image © Emma Kohlmann
"Bust" [detail] (2013), watercolor on paper.

All City Lights Books are distributed to the trade by
Consortium Book Sales and Distribution: www.cbsd.com

For small press poetry titles by this author and others,
visit Small Press Distribution: www.spdbooks.com

City Lights Books are published at the City Lights Bookstore,
261 Columbus Avenue, San Francisco, CA 94133
www.citylights.com

To all the girls

ACKNOWLEGMENTS

Portions of this book appeared as chapbooks published by Poor Claudia and Ecstatic Peace Library. Many poems were first published in the following journals and magazines: *Art Papers, BlazeVOX, Elimae, Jubilat, La Petite Zine, OMG, Octopus Magazine, NADA Contemporary Poetry Zine, NOÖ Journal, Peacock Online Review, The Poetry Project Newsletter, Sea Ranch*, and *Sixth Finch*. The poems *You Don't Know How to Make Love, Asperity*, and *Negative Desire* were included in the anthology *It's Night in San Francisco but it's Sunny in Oakland* (Timeless, Infinite Light, 2014). Many thanks to the editors.

So much gratitude to Emma Borges-Scott, Jane Gregory, Ally Harris, Kit Schluter, Paige Taggart, Bridget Talone, and Cassandra Troyan for their consideration of this manuscript. Thank you to my friends, family, and many teachers, for everything.

CONTENTS

WOMEN IN PUBLIC

NEGATIVE DESIRE

There is nothing wrong
with being sensitive.
I just want to say that
there is nothing wrong.
I make myself into a line.

I have on no outfit
when I'm waiting for you
in the wings.
Intelligence is loose,
like I'm a blind thing,
your baroque wet
lips are telling
me a number:
One.

Good luck
is mostly innuendo.
We are having sex
and all that I can think of

is how easy
it would be to kill you.
Eyes turn in
to one black box
and that is when

The horror of myself
and the meanness of myself.
The black boxes of my body
floating just above the earth.

THE PAINTING IN MODERN LIFE

I watch the men show
muscles through the trees.

Their hairless chests
reflecting sunlight, slow as glass

they walk transparent and return
each time to the same point.

On the other hand,
I rush to be unwise.

A blot of ink blacks
out my stomach, still

button of a clock,
a set of teeth perched

on a camera stand,
a plastic chalice.

I don't give a fuck
about the sun.

I only have eyes for
blow up dolls.

I put pomade on my sternum,
winding up the saddle

as a hairless Siamese
lays scratching in its corner.

While we're stacked and straddling
the branch, I whisper

Right now my vagina is closer
to your ass than it is to mine.

and it is true. Isn't that the way
love's supposed to be?

A blurry shadow of a group of people,
moving all together.

I'm a girl and I'm a woman.
And a boy and a baby

and a motorcycle.
And a fuzzy, greenish picture of Jesus.

I contain my piss into the helmet,
begging you to watch me

tracing skulls above your head,
emojis whistle like a flame

He's a rebel I was blind.
He's a rebel now he's mine.

I understand that my agenda
made this awkward.

I meant it only as an act
of aesthetic interference.

Don't you get it?
My single insurrection in this life
is my fertility.

Yesterday, I polished seven pairs of boots.
It was really something.

SELF-LOVE / THE EMPRESS

I hate sleeping because
then I cannot keep improving

I don't think there's anything
the matter with ambition

My betterness or worseness
is not a part of the public domain

I'd like to fuck myself so hard
I get pregnant and give birth to me

I'll say daddy was a bad man
I'll say mama was his bag man

But I'll take care of little me so good
I'll make myself fried eggs

ADULT ACNE

In the damp sick
In the dough
In the chewed on chew of faces
of expensive car owner faces
chewed ons of the world:
I do not fetishize the truth
I poke around
Holding my bland sandwich
in my non-dominant hand, I think
what could be worse, I think
what could be as bad?

To feel the thing you want
to feel and not to care

To be a wet road
in the dark

I'd like to thank
Toyota, like to thank

my parents, esthetician
Ritalin Clonazepam internet TV weed
my beautiful dresses

I THOUGHT ABOUT IT SO IT MUST HAVE HAPPENED

Red bright jam
on soft white bread

I unbutton my shirt
and am awakened
by what makes me sick

Light fuzz in broken hair
Lying holds the pleasure
of ruining a form
Life
will wake you up

Watching a cock
get its throat slit
blood runs in
to thin white cup
How beautiful I felt then

Lips
like earthworms

Every observation is perverse
So kiss me
like you're eating
soft serve
from a cone

9.7

When it is not enough to be I cross the vent.
I pigeon toed and stinking
from the inconsistent climate
cross
and it is done.

When I across the vent
am better than I know that
better than I know that
you can love me better
than the once rare daisy
I do not believe *deserves*
yet hope springs interest
fragile as a macaroni brain
and the hamburger of the brain
and the orange of the floor of the brain.

All our similarities are boring.
We are not reborn
we are reborn in situ.

Born with perfume, born with a timorous
kiss pumped tight on both our souls
are dented dents reflecting Andalusian depressive poise.
When it is done.
When who is there.
When cross I cross
the umber grain save open
loops of chain my love
attends to good and bitter
every night our chances twist+lasso long
+cord approximation 1+cord+vibrate
1+1+series of the crowd
2 horrors of our de toilette is bored
when who is there
when it is done
when who is there is done
and done
I cross
and stink.

BY THE TIME I ARRIVED

He spent hours
mouthing as he chewed
His hands smelled like ketchup
I wanted to wipe them
on the clean braid
of the beautiful woman
who had sat beside us

Mouthing as he opened up
the packet nursing
folds to tiny noses
he is waiting
for a call
but I
will fuck
the face
of any man
who looks
away

Glove eyes leave you
nothing special

A painting of a tongue
covered in sand
needs no explanation
I will run
my fingers
through your dark
fermenting hair

This is a blank spot
a black fricative slowly repeating
and I do work and he does nothing

LIKE THE SHADOW OF A BOAT

Like the shadow of a boat
I am a huge girl

You won't degrade me
with your pesky notes of enervation

I put my hair down
over my eyes
until I'm dumb

We look nothing alike

I put my wet hair
in front of my wet
eye, whisper, you feel good

I drag my big, wet hand
across my big, heavy body

If I have one thing to confess
then it is all I meant

In Marseille
I am cutting myself
out of a piece of paper

The font swims at me
a serif font
a dozen peaches bobbing in the sink

Solitude
stillness and solitude

Though faint of public heart
I can see the refuse
in your eyes

As you fan the public showcase with your sleeve
when you are not here

YOU DON'T KNOW HOW TO MAKE LOVE

Your voice
like a fish
is okay

It casts itself as reason
or not

There are whole universes on the internet
you have never even heard of

You talk
your quick talk
of incursion
between two
halves of the brain
which are star-like
and without saliva

I want to drain
the clear batteries of your eyes

but, on the verge of being violent
I become lazy

You need a woman
who does her shopping on the "web"

Which does kill people
in Korea
and in my mind
where I am looking at a picture of Marlene Dietrich

We have specialized beyond reason

It stuns my stupid head
still ringing with the deluge
of having a body

I do not wish
I lay down
I truly do believe
in jerking off

I may look like a real woman
but my narrating voice
has a long, white beard

GOOSE

In the woods with one hand. Last
year not now not spotless. Glands.
Splendid circle they leak. Stare and
foam and sheep-sweat. Love selves
on the body. Sleeves and bend.
Growing old is the fanciest. Off.
Comes deep. Never like a minute.
The calf. Cowling a minute comes.
Deep cover. Salt beds. You are one
of those women. Mashed. A
sonnet. Speak plainly of things
pubic. It is beautiful. It is the
square of beautiful. Contrite and
metal. Figurine.

Grade school wore you duct tape hard so much in common last year
I'm bored stumble homeblind masturbation. Sycophant, I press the
pus from your nipple.

Red wax lips cover your lips and between your teeth you shake in the
bath even kill what you had meant to trap.

Earth of pupils iris the ground.
Children run towards waves. Nice
as a different kind of rude. You
have lost your hands. The pupil of
the earth. Tongue and whine and
teeth fall out at banquet fortune
bows. The tourniquet. To
alabaster.

To desire is to be unquiet
but my desire's to be silent.

LOVE MOM

A word meaning nothing
like what it sounds
crepuscular has to do with dim
light or things
at twilight
like animals that are active at those times
bunnies are
crepuscular feeders
strange word

BE A FRIEND

Fortune faked you
snuck you from the dinner table
silent as a fold
how red your face
is raw meat red

Your carved-in Appalachian Becky voice
and Becky, I have never talked in mine

You are still
eleven, Becky
two hot bruises
when you shake
your hair
has never been more sure
and you are nearly old

You think beauty
is a good thing
to forgive

Just because
your parents had you, Becky
had to so you wouldn't have to
have you, with your shirt pulled up
your thumb print pressed
the TV red if you are
lucky, Becky I will make you
feel like you are lucky

Your smile like a finger

What is pleasing to me
is what I cannot mind

ZOOM SEQUENCE

Time is a mouth
a toothy orifice
stretched light across the hung on
summer blown glass bawd of
bulb dark twinning sweeps and seepfalls
licked into an ear

Repeating spirals interrupted
flesh of radial music
made flesh reduced to flood
of parallel twirl the toad it was
a mouth breeder
beams to cumshine bright
pennies on the city street

GOD WAS THE WAY IT WAS

Was born a dog-girl
instant hit turned hot
fucking a candle in the bathroom
a body falling out of itself

Was born a red sweater face
a dog, a girl, a girl-girl
it happens on you
dad says you could be in playboy

GLUTTON THE SESTINA

FOR HAYLEY

We gluttonous with sound, depress the line
to lively stand its silky trousered fit
whence piggly, schoolyard fuck with awkward speed
great tallow horse's eye to fallowed quit

Good horse eye, grader, backward to be shucked
an oily shove retainer's tired fit
fluke ragamuffin, warp to ply her top
yarn yellow bowl to book and just don't quit

Dear scarecrow hair, your scar and fat, dear flim
your fair faced hair is looped with slimy grit
lisps manic in reflexive song of mine
his horse eye loved to have a mom so fit

Must vest our selves so finely pig lives past her prime or horse will
guillotine poor piglet's gut for twine

> Listen miss
> this world could be
> your livery dove
> your glov-ed pigeon
> dripping *le bon* air

WOMEN IN PUBLIC

Once upon a time
Saint Bernadette was born
first child of her mom
A homely woman
of absurd virtue
she had the martyr's squint
of a Bernadette

A purple saint
an asthmatic saint
of course, she suffered much
What does the world hate more
than women
in public

When I am in my robe
then I am like a mom

I do well in bed
and do not wait

When I look in the mirror
and my face is everywhere

All you cult born infants
think the earth is your clarinet
and like to crawl across its body

Do you think that you are greater than a mom?

When it is so hot
I lie on the floor

When I think
of what I have
to give

Life has it's good points

And the fat, white thigh-bones
of a tourist

Dear mom
beautiful mom

Smile, as you always have
and ask me what I need

Remember
I'm your prisoner

LULLABYE

I like to eat the same foods all the time
and imagine all the other foods are made of plastic

When the whole world is made of plastic
the whole world is smiling with you

EVERYTHING FEELS IMPORTANT
TO A TINY PERSON

When my car got towed
you lent me the money
but were kind of an asshole

We waited in the impound lot
I stuck the toe of my sneaker
into a puddle
it was the color of fish

Tonight I rubbed cream on your ass
it felt worthwhile
though not exactly great

You told me a story
about New Jersey
I had many different thoughts
and they were all great
I guess what I am saying is

If I baked you a pie
you would sweat
while you ate it
with your perfect lips

WILD AT HEART

If I could be anything other than the dinner table, I would be the kitchen rag. I say and I look at your face. And the side of your face. You would never keep me warm. I just know. The plastic bag of your neck, you don't love me, and even though I have thighs that could slap the shit out of a leather couch, you don't think that I am funny. Listen, I'm not political, I am distracted. When I think about you. And our kid and the litter. And our fucked up parents and our promising careers. When I look at you. When I am cutting your hair in my mind.

CLOWN, GRIMACER, FLOORMAT, YESMAN, ENTERTAINER

Oh you swimming public
be a friend
swish that public
slide again
your public dorsal white things
on the muggy
sedan floor

Trash is power
trash is open
is my field is I feel
dirty in your eyes
yet indivisible our fat

Saying you are good
is not the same
as being good

But is it proof that I don't love you?

All you men of no good feeling
be forewarned
your animals resent you

They clench their jaws
and call their moms
so many times a day

HOW MANY PEOPLE ASK

I am not one whole thing
but the fear of not knowing
who will be the next
is like a blindness

Jerking off at night
I think about the difference
my bathroom's peach
twin brothers working out

I do not adore this obligation
or myself

ALL NATURAL

AFTER HANNAH WILKE

It goes in
with a shape of its own
and comes out
as real garbage

Bloodsucker
off the night
Homer of your bod

I have water up my nose

What gives you to me?

Your ballet slipper, pink
your brain your bubble
pink your junk
it works its mouths
all natural

If we are the plastic
so we are the bug

That eats the puzzle
that has the disease
that doesn't watch

Question:
What makes shit nature?

Answer:
Nature shits

Does nature warm the earth?
I care
to dig your natural warmth
your natural highs
and love the shit you make
with your mind/body shit

Your body:
A story the mind tells itself.

Your mind:
Made out of body.

Plastic body
body body blah
blah blah

Oh baby, baby
even maggots must be cute
to a maggot lady

WHO INVENTED ME

Looming like a leg pile
today is learning to be sturdy
Sissies fuck and run for it
Whip their heads around

Pears are the healthiest shape for a body
science says
Harry & David say, says

A man, another man, or was it
me who puked carrots into the bowl
is hardiness a different kind of frigid
I am still committed, frankly

I'll sit lower on my hips
relax my heaviness into the floor
press a Jesus sticker
upon the cheek of my enemy

A VOLUPTUOUS DREAM DURING AN ECLIPSE

Rotten, he says, motherly
how could you miss that

Like a ragamuffin with no eyes
his body has a dark spot

Like doing laundry all day long
he is being nowhere

Cottage cheese runs out his mouth

Another one and another one
that doll can crawl
his insides like an awning

Motherly if mother
mother as if spread

If I could break
the hymen of his ear with
I can't stand you

I won't say a thing and I won't notice
god you are
the softest
kind of jerk
and yesterday is gone
and I had nothing to do with it

YESTERDAY IS GONE AND I HAD NOTHING
TO DO WITH IT

I squat
like a frog
in a warm peel of light
spider veins and teeth
golden
presidential teeth

I think
about taking
a vacation

Mostly, things are dull
and summer drops
in fertile blades

THE WAY THEY ACT THE WAY THEY DRESS

Steeple blond
your mask askew and stapled
at the temple

What a pair
to blubber in the mirror

What a pair
to rattle on your chest

Love's delivery
is a temporary gentle
underwhelming as a sleeping pill

Your full eyes slack
their poodly plastic clap
roll bedroom high

They sky the sky
the high high high

SEA BIRDS END THE NAKED SEA. AND ME.
AND ME.

I am in the market
for a tiny organ
and a pair of jeans

I can feel
how they will feel
casing my body

I will slide them on
I will pull them off

On TV a pretty
blond girl gives
someone the softest kiss
I can taste her mouth
taste through the screen
Her halcyonic thigh
I close my eyes
into the sucking blue

Help
my radio
is broken and the world
is so unfair
I'm going to fuck
myself to blame
I only have myself

Sometimes,
when I'm lying
on the floor,
I think of physics

A perfect toaster
sitting on the street
To hold my cum
I do not cum
and do not think
How to the world I am
the way my stare is
How I cracked the code
of online dating

Monday, I'm balloons
at race's finishing
Friday swoons away
The time flies
winnowing

HAVING NEVER READ ADORNO

I understand myself
only insofar
as it is funny

IN BED, WITHOUT ELSA, STRUM

Light-pour warms my guts
so pleasingly chromatic
sun dilates your face
piss soft into the shower

Is it bad that I'm not interested in
"what life means," etc.
you'll find out when you get there
that's what I say

The peach-of-the-temple-of-your-throat-your
breath is how many dollars
Elsa, come
does it always have to be
about "the process"

No one likes to sound abandoned, Elsa
love my guts as I do yours
divine yet inexpensive
fortune is soft bodied

It is best not to transform
rather: irritate and signal

Elsa, I may sleep in trash
but in my dreams
your tongue is in my mouth
is swollen as a toe, courageous
Elsa of my dreams

IMP, IMP

In a house filled with machines
in the deep flit of your eyes
boldly rolling, high as a fruit pallet

Your voice, your voicely voice
how many Elsas fit in one dark box?

My little enemy
this is a serious Tuesday
I'm as healthy as a boy for you

AUTUMN

These particular mansions
they lay out

They have no sound
but the slight hiss of their giant ranges
hissing in their marble kitchens
and their giant trees
exposing nothing
do not hiss

More than a man
more than my love
more than the oubliette
of some decision

for New England
I'm disarmed

I blink
with the cloudless

eyes of a beagle
at these norm fucks
with the limp dicks
of a hundred thousand
geezers in their sleep

This is a big house
it does not owe itself
another brilliant night
yet, I am at the party

Without the sea
to crash against my genitals
or the veil of a beautiful day
or the tall Dutch Elm

THE LAMP SHADE IS SITTING BADLY
ON ITS LAMP

But: you again, you
—I mean outside me
you are not drunk
and I am not alone

FRANCIS BACON

I said to Francis Bacon
you are a worm in public
a worm in bed
head first in the blankets, squealing
I know that was you

My eyes have a mouth
my ear has a windshield
look at that stick bug
it has eyes
everything is the same

This is such a Presbyterian planet
moving from pattern to inconsequence—
there is a painting of my face
behind my face

Nose like a tortilla chip
nose like a mushroom nose

like a piece of glass against the rain
and the nose of my cervix

And how the coldest part of the ocean
is not the most strange

And how thinking about one thing
is the same as thinking about another

I LOVE THE BEACH

We possess nothing in this world other than the power to say "I."
This is what we must yield up to God.

—Simone Weil

I call out from the water perfectly
oh hello glossolalia my God
the great flat grays and shimmies

Pacific spanks up to my chest
Nicole says this is temporary
oh everything but stillness still

Naaman's on the blanket
tells me to get lost
I scrawl and scrawl yield nothing

God says this is temporary
says you're a contact lens for Me to gaze through
He looks backwards through my mouth

God sees me sucking on a tendril
I stick my tongue into the sand
I write and scrawl

Elsewhere Naaman shimmy stoops to sick
sick slicks across my blanket
oh my God Nicole says get away

Elsewhere I rub sand across my body
I am giggle-choking on the scald
lopped off

VENTRILOQUIST

At the last of one's patience
anyone can be so quiet

IT TAKES A REAL MAN TO BE A LITTLE GIRL

FOR COCO

In the middle of the night
in an eclipse
in that cereal box of darkness
I stand, a man who hates men
and almost all women

Instead of having a body
I would like a t-shirt of a body
a big, sensual t-shirt
luscious jersey knit
and very quiet

But you, love
you are lovely as a tube of lip gloss
chin barged out like a beer gut
your embryonic wheeze
a glow stick in a tree

when all the lunch girls screamed
you screamed the softest

There is so much I don't understand
even more I do not want to know
but you, love, when you hold me
when you lay me fast asleep
so plush and fathered in your couch
any fool can die

and the whole world stares

LET IT ALL GO ON WITHOUT ME

You think beauty
is a good thing
to forgive

Smile like a finger

What is pleasing to me
is what I cannot mind

IN FRANCE, THE GIRLS SLEEP IN BLUE EYESHADOW

You tell me to get in bed
to turn the light on
your skin like a soft paper bag
your lips like two soft paper bags

I'm lonely, I say
I hated that dinner

I know, you say

Light falls down
like we are in two
canopy beds

WHAT IS TRUE IS THE WAY THINGS ARE

In my mind I'm swimming
towards you
Thighs hemmed by cold
water, oval, double-oval
Hem and slice and slice.

I drag a wet dark
hem across your lips
Finger press the wool
against your tongue

In my mind you give a little
penetration of the netting

Water is the supernatural
I wallow in
become half-strange and
shove into my skirt

WATCHING IT HAPPEN

I laze about, deranged and unafraid
to godly kiss you, kiss the pharmacist
that whipped you, undilute, to dilate high
your animus of lime and lye.

I know of an upstairs hell.
A creamy, vascular thump
through bonus years of things that pass
and things that do not move.
Your cellular mouth. Your mess
of inattention. Now that none
of us are good looking I think
that/they are right.

Strokes of light you taped across my nipple.
Patterns staked to fake the love
we cannot feel so slick the miser
of your hand through my bad heart.

Genius, you are blond enough.
Once in a while.

And in the end, when I sweep coolly up
and will not be drawn back,
then I will tell you of it. How I can.
In writing, I am making an attempt
to depict my beautiful nose
through imagery.

I will tell you of it. Once in a while.
I will miss you. And the tape.
To be flung down,
petals from a balcony.

VISIONING

Fakes   their black tongues are reaching out
Fakes   their golden hands are in the water   their hands are
cuffed behind your back
your god is a triangle between
yes and Fakes   their guardian dogs
have got you pounding against the udder of a tree

Tadpoles slid into you
dog-faced urchins have
piled upon your body   made soup of your itch
but you know how it is to curl your fingers
what is there to touch but risk, anyway

I wouldn't be so sure of this
if I were not prepared to strip

Today I sat with my legs apart all day

SO, THEN

I could be crystallized
spread like a young
mother I could buzz
the fungus clear off

SIXTY FIVE PERCENT OF WHAT I THROW AWAY
IS COMPOST

I get high and eat
all seven cara cara
oranges, I read/listen
say refrains like
Psyche err her sin
was mostly playing
what the camera tells you
writing is a form of
throwing out

The bunnies and the poets
we are born to die
before the king
perpetually chilled out
by thin-lipped
boys with pretty hands
they can't deceive me
I can see he has
the pristine middle

part of someone
who's in pain

Define *jouissance* as easy
menstrual cycles
back to back
upcycled heat
in refilled toner's
small perplexing dream
of voltage high
enough to generate
the mediocrity
from which I run, now
is it more offensive
to insist on being seen
or to reject visibility at all?
Babe, if you really loved me
you would jump

What is indestructible? by Ezra Pound
Que Sera, Sera by Doris Day
You remember the time
when we fell in—tell me

should I wait
or should I live?

Lit within that atrium's
unperfect star

Arranged
so strange to fall apart

So closely to
the way it claimed to be

like Artemis
I am no fun

Still typing fast
into the whacking spray, hey

I don't want to matter to you
I just want to cost

Oh baby/ please/ release me/ to my knees
to the sound/ of cue balls/ knocked together

CHICK FILLET

Monica pukes out
the gentlest font of sick
that I have ever seen
and I can have no other
thought but how
thought but how
the flat white tops of waves
can have no other
thought but how

We hate this freedom
don't we?
We were young
and I was had
to rub my body
on the world's
young eyebrows
Ocean flaps
a canvas tent
To be in such a state

of self-possession
there can be
no other master
Yesterday I planned
on pulling out my hair

I have known
this fast to cultivate
a certain sharpness
I have known
myself to kneel
at what has yet
forgot to have
no other thought
but how
to say Elaine
or Monica
or Ally
or Nicole
or Clare

TO MOUTH THE MOUTH

Irradiant, irradiating circlet
a chilly heave, the thorough current
of an antithetical Mute Swan
lengthening the Arabian Crawl to her doorstep
then disappeared inside a branch

She squawks and panders, lisps
the already-of-her-night clings to its furnace
giantly plumaged in rivulets of sweat
and three opal stars

YOUR JOKE IS A LAKE, YOUR RULE BLEW UP
A GAS STATION

Dead birds fly around
They're looking
happy for me, she said
Life is shit but you are chaste
Ring-ring-a-ding Hello
your face is the alarm
so laugh because this pain is common
wait because it won't demand
now let me suck your cock
atop the doctor's burning car

Well, what does one possess
but all their many selves?
What does one admit
but incapacitation?

I will find the bondage
of your qualities
will wait with pigtails

tied to track lights
I'll disqualify
this night
from ever being had

You are pretty
as a prick
and you are real
as a real bell
but I would ransom
all awareness
for a sturdy floor

And though it's true
our sex is cosmic
I could fuck a star

IN LIFE WE ARE THE STORIES THAT WE TELL ABOUT OURSELVES

Say a field trip summer roller rink and Annie ugly so was I the bleachers cotton pink a wilted pink a tear of snot across my bag the smell of crawl her forehead smell of Annie's pad her chest hair worms I lied the plastic water Annie she says thrumming Annie talks the screen door porch and in the glass I lied the van the floor she moved it kind of pink and jealous even pictures have a kid still slowly pricking Annie in the bathroom stall a brick a wall a crying bottle I have scrubbed my legs my marker badness little boys who swimming pool the lungs I have a feeling Annie told me scrubbed my legs say field trip summer roller rink and Annie so the bleachers pink a cotton pink a tear of snot her head smell crawl of Annie's pad her chest hair thrumming on the tub the van the floor the Sunday park whose reckless move in boys in even pictures say a bottle up to swim to swim with marker legs still pricking Annie in a stall to heave my chin my water brains and scrubs when what was left of sponges summer brain and I do not remember sidelong eaves I say a field trip summer roller rink with Annie ugly so the bleachers cotton pink a tear of snot a wilted pink the smell of Annie's pad her head smell bleachers marker legs her pricking water reckless sponge of summer brains a field trip summer crawl of bleachers pink and wilted tear my bag my smell my forehead smell the crawl

of Annie's pad her chest hair in a stall my chin to heave to pink and
sick against the cotton jealous I and smell the summer crawl of field
trip chest hair love my pricking legs

        I do not remember
        what was left
        or what the summer banged against

WATER, LIGHTNESS, PUBERTY. TIREDNESS. SHUT.

Mom says it is not a good idea
to feel too good about yourself

The feeling of getting what you want
is the feeling of nothing
she says
Be productive

JACK & DIANE

Only the hind-parts and plastic
eyes in your rabbity face
I am the wife I love to punch
to sully your marvel with a thin con
I am the King of Jokes
doubled-over with triumph

Husband, swelter has nutrition
and I, the normal wife
of your punctured eyes
fawn over the toilet

Ask a normal question
your dirty jokes aren't miracles
in my opinion
no desire is benign

Yet, in the pilled-out spell of night
when what I think of is the pills
in all the pockets

in all the trench coats in the world
I will sway like a swinging babe
and you will think it was the pills
and I will go to sleep

THE MYTH OF THE FEMALE ORGASM

Winter runs into rubbery toothpaste
 winter   rubs
on how we stand there
no one honest ever cared

From   in   between our thighs streamed fertile shattering desires
of anyone whose cares we couldn't stand

No one honest
sticks against our bank of chest

and when we talked about it
our lips touched
and we were faking it

ASPERITY

Roughness of surface; unevenness
in rough places; excrescences

The asperities of dry bodies
The asperities of the moon

Roughness to the taste; sourness; tartness
Roughness or harshness of sound
that quality which grates
upon the ear; raucity
Roughness of literary style.

Roughness to the feelings; disagreeableness
rigor; hardship; difficulty; bleakness; inclemency
The nakedness and asperity of the wintry world
Roughness of manner or of temper;
tartness; severity; crabbedness

It is no very cynical asperity
not to confess obligations
where no benefit has been received

WILL MY LOVE BE LAME

My mind has on no cloak
but I am more.
Each day I'm more
a grave
becoming leaky green.

Parts with branches, parts with impositions.
Parts more insolent
more solemn, more awake.
Should I let this farce of peace
arcane and un-emphatic
tie me to my chair?

Life imagines me
to be benign
but I am randomly dementing.
What I feel
is my own free death
and my own free life.

One more dose
to dress the golden homer
pursed against my own eroding face.

If given to entomb
just know
that sweetness lies
within that tomb
in every pretty spray.

I do not say
my calling
is the same as what I choose;
I pit my mind against
the vaguest port
more terrible
than even thoughts
I choose to sound.

I KNOW I AM NOT AN EASY WOMAN

I have seen a million
pictures of my face
and still
I have no idea

MILK

A father is the enemy
of what is sensual
When my father, then my dad
when love created woman
made her own dead eyes
and this is how to end a man

Dish soap, popcorn, jelly flats
Why take time when action
is what moves me
As you sleep I touch your neck
and I'm relieved
when you do not wake up

You say
to know me is to smile
Though my soul's a bandaged hand
a letter saying sorry slowly
spilled by some mistake, the ocean
purity is unalloyed

so I pull down my pants
to give it to the sea

Baby is a soothing word
it slides across my tongue
so blunt and long and verdant
a regular arousal, firm
I get drunk and buy a donut
pleasure is your birthright
the receipt tape says
I bought it, *Baby*
now it's ours
cuz god does not exist
and nature doesn't care
and we are here
so why not break the chart

I will lie to feel with you
I'll run the rivers dry with you
to curl up in the curl
of your good touch

I crank myself and sigh
Baby
you listen and he dies

NAME LIKE AN EMPTY BAG

My house is a mess. Fuck. Fuck. I burned my
sweater on the stove. The smell of melted
acetate, of reading. What if I hate
it just because she does a better job
of being me than I do? Too familiar,
the sound of keeping my mouth closed.

I am wearing cycling gloves. I'd like everyone
to put down their bran muffin for a
moment and consider the peace that comes
from staring into the eyes of dog.
Everybody needs someone to be themselves
around. But the moonlight is not the moon.

Better people buck the sentimental
fake of body I'm no rust or green me
gulp, I gotta. I will let my hair grow
greasy, I am just a woman with her
arms crossed. Feeling better than I was more
quickly than expected. That is usual.

How you come up from a nap and fear
that you will never truly be awake
again. Bed sheets, blankets, Joan-of-Arc-like
clothing, lamp, a ring. The material
fishhook does not cease to be a sex act
don't be foolish when I tell you

I have loved you just the way you are.
I always wanted to die of consumption.
Nothing truer than a McRib or a
double rainbow. I put garbage in my pockets.
Read a book. Write a letter. Thank you for
the object, for the attitude of grace.

The world is much more tolerant of the
anorectic female head-case. Bravery,
O boring masochism. I will beg
you for your patience, trust, my weirdness
is a side-effect of trying to be
normal, swear, I do my best, loins,
I've grown tired of girding you.

Despite I
Empty out I
Sleeping out I

I am attracted to me?
It is fun to sit in me?

I finish the book.
I throw the book away.

The state of the world calls out for poetry
to save it. LAWRENCE FERLINGHETTI

CITY LIGHTS SPOTLIGHT SHINES A LIGHT ON THE WEALTH
OF INNOVATIVE AMERICAN POETRY BEING WRITTEN TODAY.
WE PUBLISH ACCOMPLISHED FIGURES KNOWN IN THE
POETRY COMMUNITY AS WELL AS YOUNG EMERGING POETS,
USING THE CULTURAL VISIBILITY OF CITY LIGHTS TO BRING
THEIR WORK TO A WIDER AUDIENCE. IN DOING SO, WE ALSO
HOPE TO DRAW ATTENTION TO THOSE SMALL PRESSES
PUBLISHING SUCH AUTHORS. WITH CITY LIGHTS SPOTLIGHT,
WE WILL MAINTAIN OUR STANDARD OF INNOVATION AND
INCLUSIVENESS BY PUBLISHING HIGHLY ORIGINAL POETRY
FROM ACROSS THE CULTURAL SPECTRUM, REFLECTING
OUR LONGSTANDING COMMITMENT TO THIS MOST
ANCIENT AND STUBBORNLY ENDURING FORM OF ART.

CITY LIGHTS SPOTLIGHT

1

Norma Cole, *Where Shadows Will:*
Selected Poems 1988-2008

2

Anselm Berrigan, *Free Cell*

3

Andrew Joron, *Trance Archive:*
New and Selected Poems

4

Cedar Sigo, *Stranger in Town*

5

Will Alexander, *Compression & Purity*

6

Micah Ballard, *Waifs and Strays*

7

Julian Talamantez Brolaski, *Advice for Lovers*